97 ways to make a
Dog Smile

97 ways to make a
Dog Smile

BY JENNY LANGBEHN
PHOTOS BY PAT DOYLE

WORKMAN PUBLISHING · NEW YORK

Library of Congress Cataloging-in-Publication Data
Langbehn, Jenny.
97 ways to make a dog smile / by Jenny Langbehn ; photos by Pat Doyle.
p. cm.
ISBN-13: 978-0-7611-2903-5
1. Dogs. 2. Dogs Pictorial works. 3. Smile. I. Title: Ninety seven ways to make a dog smile. II. Title.

SF427.L268 2003
636.7'0022'2--dc21   2003041143

Workman books are available at special discounts when purchased in bulk for premiums and sales
promotions as well as for fund-raising or educational use. Special editions or book excerpts can also
be created to specification. For details, contact the Special Sales Director at the address below.

Workman Publishing Company, Inc.
225 Varick Street
New York, NY 10014-4381
www.workman.com
Printed in U.S.A.
First printing April 2003
10 9

Dedication

For two of the finest people ever to grace the planet:
my parents, Pam and Roger.
Through them I learned the importance of respecting
those that can't necessarily speak for themselves.
They encourage me in all things, and have never begrudged
me the occasional batch of orphaned creatures.
I love you both very much.

Introduction

Dogs are extraordinary creatures. Each has his or her own distinct personality; and like the proverbial snowflake, no two are just alike. Loyal and flirtatious, placid and rambunctious, ready for a marathon play session and then quietly and comfortably nestled on the sofa, they live to please and seem to do so with great joy. This drive to please is unique among animals; no other creature is so motivated by its guardian's happiness. And in the face of that kind of devotion, it's impossible to not want to reciprocate.

As all dog lovers know, dogs will delight in even the simplest activities. I find this one of their most enchanting and endearing qualities. Every walk is thrilling. Every car ride brings the possibility for adventure. Each rub is so pleasurable it simply must not end! Even a makeshift toy, like an old sock, can be extraordinarily fascinating each and every time it is played with. It is so easy and so much fun to make your dog happy—so happy that he or she actually smiles—that it makes the continuous mission to think up new and invigorating ways to please your pooch a natural extension of your love. The 97 ways suggested in these pages are just a few of the infinite possibilities for having fun.

The rubs, tickles, games, tricks, and treats that I include here are tried and true favorites that have worked for my own dogs, and many of the dogs that I have come to know over the years. I am pleased to report that many of my tricks of the trade have made the veterinary appointments of numerous dogs (and their people) that much more pleasant. (In fact, quite a few patients actually look forward to their visits!) Most activities developed from the simple act of diversion from an unpleasant procedure, and evolved into one of sheer fun and unadulterated joy. Of course, not every suggestion is right for every dog. Many factors like breed, temperament, and age will affect a dog's reaction. Pay close attention to any activity your dog is enthusiastic about, and skip anything that makes him or her seem uncomfortable.

My hope is that this book will be the springboard for a lifelong plan of creative and bonding exercises in fun for you and your dog. I would love to hear about your experiences with the activities in this book as well as any fun that results from them. Feel free to write me at doggiesmile@aol.com.

1. Lower-Ear Noogies

A tried-and-true massage location,
the ears are very sensitive sites. At the base of
the ear, gently rub your knuckles in true noogie
fashion. (To make a noogie, form a half fist
with your knuckles sticking out.)

2. Inner-Ear Noogies

Put your hand in noogie position, and with the
knuckle of your middle finger, rub the little piece
of cartilage that juts out at the entrance to the
inside of your dog's ear. The dog's head will
probably tilt to one side, with her eyes half closed.

3. You are getting very sleepy. . . .

Using your index finger, slowly stroke the bridge of the nose in the direction the hair grows.

4. Using both hands, gently knead (don't pinch!)

the excess skin of your dog's back and scruff. Sing a rousing rendition on "That's Amoré" as you knead the dog's skin like pizza dough.

5. Make a "hand" sandwich.

When your dog is lying on his side, slip your hand between him and the floor (starting at the shoulder), and run your hand slowly along the length of his body. The ripple will result in canine ecstasy. Doggie will probably roll onto the flat of his back, which means you can do this again using both hands—one on each side.

NOTE: Try this with your foot if the dog doesn't mind foot pats.

6. The Jell-O Mold

For our portly friends, place one hand (palms flat) on either side of the dog's body and gently shake the flesh. Optional sound effects include: a whirring noise or the Jell-O gelatin jingle ("Watch it wiggle, see it jiggle . . .").

7. The Thumper

Cupping your hand slightly, use your fingertips
to rapidly scratch your dog on her side,
just where the ribs end. Be prepared for the foot
that may involuntarily waggle and thump
in classic bunny fashion.

8. Locate all of the cowlicks

in the various places on your dog's coat, and trace them in a spiral motion with your index finger. Go with the grain for a soothing effect, against it to create shivers of excitement.

9. The Full-Body Massage

Starting at the snout, thoroughly and methodically massage the entire length of her body.

10. The White-Glove Massage

For a simple variation on more standard
massages, try your usual process with a pair
of socks on your hands. The sensation is quite
different for the dog because you are
covering much more surface area with
each stroke, and because your hands look funny
with socks on them.

11. Scratch *under* your dog's collar.

Most petting skips over this vital spot,
but many dogs fall over in pure rapture when
this area is addressed.

12. The Instant Face-Lift

Using the palms of both hands, smooth the skin
of the cheeks gently back in stroking motions
toward the neck. This action has been described
as eliciting a "false grin," but I assure you
that the smile is genuine.

*NOTE: I like to accompany this move with commentary in my best
Zsa-Zsa Gabor voice: "Dahlink, you look vanderful."*

13. Dogs have very expressive eyebrows.

In some cases, the brows differ in color from the rest of the facial hair. These spots are extremely relaxing massage points.
Rub the eyebrows gently in small circles, being careful not to poke the dog's eye.

14. El Matador

Some dogs love the romance and pageantry
of a good old-fashioned bullfight.
Wave a towel or blanket provocatively while
shouting "Toro, Toro!" As your little hornless bull
charges, whisk the "cape" away
at the last second.

*Note: If you have cheering audience members at your disposal,
by all means employ them!*

15. Do you miss your dog while you're away?

She misses you, too! Phone home and play a message on the speaker of your answering machine. Make sure you say her name loud and clear.

16. Place your ear over your dog's chest, so that you can hear his heartbeat.

In time to your new canine metronome, serenade her with the first song that evolves from the beat.

FACT: "Duke of Earl" is by far the most common selection.

17. Woof!

Most dogs are not fooled by a human's imitation barks, but they are intrigued by them. See how good your bark (or bow-wow or howl) is by testing it on your dog. If she barks back, you are truly bilingual and the two of you can have fascinating dialogues in her native tongue. If she cocks her head and looks at you like you landed from another planet, stick to speaking English.

NOTE: This test is best performed in the privacy of your own home to avoid neighbors' stares.

18. Learn to juggle.

Or better yet, how *not* to juggle. For obvious reasons, a bad juggler is a dog's best friend!

19. Make it a Blockbuster night.

Rent the dog a nature video—specifically, a documentary about wolves. If he usually responds to TV, the sounds will inspire interest and possibly conversation with the wolves.

20. Form your own conga line.

Place your dog's paws on your waist and conga away!

*NOTE: This is best for large dogs.
Most smaller breeds prefer to dance solo.*

21. The Name Game

Who doesn't love the sound of her own name?
Say your dog's name over and over to her (Is
Maisie a good girl? Yes, *Maisie* is very nice.) and
with fun variations (Maisie, The Maiser, The
Maisinator, Miss Maiserina, Maiseroni).

22. Dogs love to outwit their people.

Pretend to "drop" a morsel of food (preferably their own), and look for the cat-that-ate-the-canary look when your dog scoops it up.

NOTE: For our canines with a conscience, this could prove torturous as they battle to resist temptation.

23. Joyride!

Hop in the car and take a spin. Crack the windows and let the wind stream through the dog's ears and fur. The windblown look is definitely in this season.

24. Towel Time

Dry off a damp dog with a towel fresh from the dryer. A warm rubdown is toasty good fun.

NOTE: Beware of static cling!

25. Give the dog a gift.

If everyone else is getting a present—
at gift-giving holidays, for example—the dog
should have one, too. Otherwise, it's not fair!
Most dogs are thoroughly excited by the
prospect of their very own package.
Just make sure that Chloë does not ingest
the wrapping as well as the treat inside.

26. Play hide-and-seek.

Hide a treat in a clever spot and see how long it takes for the dog to discover it.

27. Play the "Which Hand" game

by hiding a treat in one of your clenched fists,
and seeing if your dog will choose
the correct hand.

NOTE: Resist the urge to tease your dog by hiding nothing in either
hand. Your dog will not find this amusing.

28. Flying Saucers

Incorporate a little exercise into treat time by tossing miniature rice cakes (à la Frisbee) for your dog to chase. These low-calorie treats pack a big crunch without padding the waistline, and they are fun to catch.

29. Do you want to go for a . . . WALK?!

Say this handy phrase, then repeat "A walk! A walk!" while dancing around in front of the door.

NOTE: You must actually go for a walk after you say this.

30. Flea Pockets

Scratch the small and seemingly superfluous flaps of skin located at the base of dogs' ears. Legend has it that these are the fissures in which fleas would retreat to sleep for the evening.

31. The Aunt Martha

For our jowl-endowed friends, all of that copious
skin just begs to be pinched!
Don't forget to say, "You are just soooo cute!"
(And don't pinch too hard.)

32. The Three Little Bears routine

If you are feeling particularly silly
(and no one is looking), give your dog a huge
surprise by letting her find you curled up
in *her* bed for a change!

33. Puppy Pilates

If you do floor exercises or yoga at home, let
your dog join you on the mat.
Most dogs love to join in, especially for moves
like Downward-Facing Dog.

34. "Holy ears, Batman!"

Did you know that your floppy-eared dog does
a remarkable impression of a fruit bat?
Simply lift both ears into the upright position.
You'll be amazed by the transformation!
When the ears are in superhero formation, it's
time to play superheroes.
Take turns being hero and villain.

*Note: Some dogs are masters of disguise and can accomplish this
feat on their own by lying on their backs.*

35. Play catch.

Throw the ball; let the dog bring it back.
A classic. Mix it up with pretend throws, which
gets most dogs even more excited.
(Just actually throw the ball every now and then.)

36. Freezie Chew

Soak a doggie rope toy in water,
and then freeze it.

*NOTE: This is a great summertime treat that is also ideal for
teething puppies.*

37. The Hansel and Gretel

Leave a trail of plain popped popcorn
around the house or yard.

38. Subliminal Game

Sneak a familiar word into a long rant.
For example: "Today I was shopping in the
supermarket and I noticed that there was a spill
in the condiment aisle **cookie** and it took
nearly 10 minutes for someone to clean it up. . . . "
You may be surprised how closely your dog
actually listens to what you have to say.

*NOTE: You must provide Doggie with whatever
you have subliminally mentioned.*

39. Luke, I am your father.

Speak to your dog through the cardboard cylinder of a paper towel or wrapping-paper roll. Your dog will love your Darth Vader voice!

40. Do jumping jacks.

C'mon, everyone! One, two! One, two!

41. Hot Dogs

Rub your pooch down with a cool, wet towel.
Relief without the shock! Pay special attention to
your dog's ears and feet. Cooling these hot spots
in particular will guarantee canine comfort.
Ahhhhh!

42. Swedish Massage

Very much like your usual massage routine, only brisker, this massage is performed to the beat of your dog's favorite ABBA tune!

NOTE: Most dogs enjoy "Dancing Queen."

43. Tickle the Ivories

Play your dog's ribs like a piano keyboard.
Sing along as you practice your scales.

NOTE: Guitarists may find their dogs are built for a similar effect,
if a strumming motion is employed across the ribs.
This works particularly well in breeds with long snouts for fingering.

44. The Ham Hock

For dogs that prefer a deep-tissue massage, knead those thigh muscles as though tenderizing your main course!

45. Scratch and Sniff

It's payback time for all that sniffing you get.
The next time the dog sniffs you, sniff her back.
Make it as loud and reciprocal as you can.

*NOTE: As you may have witnessed, this behavior is perfectly
acceptable in doggie social situations, and not at all considered
rude. In fact, your dog may be touched that you made the gesture!*

46. Rubbed the Wrong Way

Pet your pup *against* the grain.

47. Pre-Game Pep Talk

This massage is performed as your dog sits in
front of you, using your thumbs to work the
muscles around your dog's scapulas (shoulders).
Great warm-up before any marathon ball
or stick chasing. Go get 'em, champ!

48. Daddy Longlegs

Form your fingers into your best spider imitation
and lightly massage your dog from head to toe.
You may notice their skin crawling,
but in a good way!

49. Wax on, Wax off

For our Zen pooches, a methodical series of
circular massage motions can induce a
meditative state that brings doggie serenity!

50. The Treat Fairy

While your dog is asleep, attempt to sneak a treat under his pillow without disturbing him. Dogs love to wake up to a surprise!

51. Go Speed Racer!

Make an obstacle course in your yard and race
the dog through it. Again! And again!

NOTE: Remember that dogs are notorious cheaters.

52. Piñata

Fill a brown paper bag with dog-friendly treats
and toys. Smack it open and watch
the sky rain Milk Bones.

53. The Hills Are Alive

It is a little-known fact that dogs love Julie Andrews (and, really, who doesn't?). Find the nearest hill or field, and with arms extended, twirl about as though you were high in the Austrian Alps. If your dog is unimpressed, you can always yodel. This ups the excitement ante considerably.

54. Bring Your Dog to Work Day

What's more exciting than a day at the office?
Nothing! New smells, new people.
No wonder you go there all the time.

*NOTE: Don't bother with W-2 forms or 401K plans,
but frequent trips to the water cooler will be appreciated.*

55. Top-Notch Massage

That bony peak atop your dog's head actually has a name: the nuchal crest. There is no real known purpose for the protuberance, but some more spiritual scholars postulate that it may be the dog's antennae for mystical energies, and should be massaged regularly for maximum reception.

56. Thoracic Park

If your dog likes to roll over,
he may not necessarily be asking for a belly rub.
Try a nice chest massage instead.

57. Parlez-Vous Chien?

Try speaking common words or commands in a different language, but use the same vocal inflection as usual. Your dog may actually understand what you mean!

58. Lazy Man's Tetherball

Not feeling particularly energetic, but still want to offer entertainment for your dog? Tie a balloon just out of reach to your ceiling fan, and let it spin.

NOTE: If your dog starts spinning out of control, this may not be the game for her. Making her dizzy is not good for her or your carpet!

59. Bobbing for Treats

Toss treats and/or toys into a shallow pool or bucket. Step back and have a mop ready.

60. Blow bubbles.

Lawrence Welk fans found soap bubbles soothing. Your dog probably finds them energizing. Watch her leap and snap.

61. Rub the kneebows.

Take a look at your dog's hocks. They aren't exactly knees; they aren't exactly elbows. Massage this funny, forgotten joint.

62. One More Set

Incorporate your dog into your workout routine
by substituting her for your hand-weights
or dumbbells! Dachshunds
(or any dogs with long torsos) work well.

63. Blind Spot

Scratch the hard-to-reach spots on the dog.
Sometimes our more chubby friends can't reach
every itch. They love it when you do.

64. Beam Me Up, Scotty

For the high-tech dog that is way beyond squeaky toys, invest in a laser pointer. This elusive quarry can jump from wall to wall, and is not bound by the physical laws of conventional balls and toys—something dogs love to hate!

NOTE: Some dogs will ignore the laser, but most develop a deep personal vendetta against their new archenemy.

65. Peanut-Butter Swirl

Place a small amount of peanut butter on the dog's tail and watch her spin like a top. This is great for an antsy dog with boundless energy and restricted space. She'll whirl away her pent-up energy, and if she ever does catch her tail, she'll have a tasty little treat!

66. Shell Game

Play the classic sleight-of-hand game, using a treat and plastic cups. Dogs have the slight advantage of being able to *smell* which of the rearranged cups is hiding the treat, but they are delighted to find it all the same.

67. Teach your dog to smile . . . literally!

Start by lifting your dog's lips to inspect his teeth and gums, all the while repeating the word "Smile!" With time, he will curl his lips back on command, and before you know it, you'll truly have a smiling dog.

68. Dogs love when you speak in rhyme.

Compose a poem in honor of your dog's traits or attributes and recite it out loud.

69. Pupsicle

The next time you are preparing an ice-cube tray, drop a kibble into each well before it freezes. How many licks does it take to get to the surprise nugget inside?

70. Hush-hush

Dogs love a good secret! Even an ordinary
statement takes on special importance when
you whisper it into your dog's ear.
Watch his reaction when you come in close
to whisper, "Go for a walk?"

71. Figaro, Figaro, Figaro!

Dogs love when you sing opera. Don't worry if you don't speak Italian; your dog will prefer that you change the words and sing about *him*.

72. It's a bird, it's a plane!

Throw a cape on and whirl around the yard like a superhero. Your dog will love being your trusty sidekick and will get a laugh out of your silly outfit.

73. Slow-mo

Dogs are fascinated by extremes. Try performing
normal activities, such as preparing a treat,
in slow motion. Tremors of anticipation
can reach 4.0 on the Richter scale.

74. Call of the Wild

Make it a ritual during each full moon
(or anytime you feel like it) to join your dog
outside for a no-holds-barred howling session.
Letting loose with a great howl is
a liberating release for *both* of you.

75. Human Hurdle

Crouch down in a doorway and throw a ball or
toy into another room. Once the toy is retrieved
and the dog makes his jaunt back toward you,
he must leap over the new barrier in
the doorway. Dogs love when they can
jump over you!

76. Bag it.

Hide your dog's favorite toy in a large brown grocery bag. Shake the bag provocatively, and let your dog root out the prize.

77. Gooaal!

A ball doesn't need to fit in your dog's mouth to be fun! Many dogs—especially herding breeds—are natural soccer players, and can expertly shuffle a large ball about with their front legs or even noses. Many dogs quickly master the keep-away objective of a good game of soccer.

78. Peek-a-boo

Even dogs find the classic game of peek-a-boo entertaining. However, unlike many children, they are not impressed with you merely hiding your face behind your hands (smart dogs). You can achieve much better effects by hiding completely beneath a blanket or sheet. Peek slyly from your hiding place and surreptitiously say her name, but watch out as she dives for your cover.

79. I Got Your Nose!

Grasp your dog's muzzle and quickly pull your cupped hand away, making a popping noise with your mouth. Many dogs get very excited by this game. (Geordie is not sure.)

80. Lord of the Rings

Still have that hula hoop stashed in your garage? Some dogs love to jump through hoops. Start with the hoop placed low to the ground, and toss a treat through. As your dog gets the idea, you can gradually raise the hoop until your pooch is leaping through the ring.

NOTE: While it is indeed dramatic, your dog will definitely not *attempt the circus version of this game with a flaming ring. So don't even think about it!*

81. The Raspberry

Okay, so this game is not for everyone. But many dogs are actually tickled by a variation on the classic "raspberry." Place your mouth over an expanse of the dog's skin, for example, near the armpit, then blow! "*Fffpppptttt!*"

NOTE: *You can even just try sticking out your tongue and making the noise. You may even get it back.*

82. Incoming!

Use a slingshot or a spoon to catapult nuggets
of kibble across the yard for your dog to pursue!

83. Cultural Heritage

Would your Viszla enjoy a polka? Would your chihuahua like to hear a mariachi band? Does your poodle appreciate the accordion? Try exposing your dog to music from his native land. If your dog has been reluctant to dance, perhaps it is simply because she didn't know the steps!

84. Piggy-Back Ride

Get down on all fours and coax your dog—
small breeds only, please!—onto your back
(this may require some help). Once your dog
is comfortable on her new human perch,
crawl around, transporting your dog around
the house or yard. This takes "going for a ride"
to a whole new level!

85. Pied Piper

Do you play the flute (or kazoo)? Can you beat out a rhythm on a drum? Use any instrument to call your dog into an impromptu musical procession, and watch her follow the leader!

86. Bowl-O-Rama

Line up your dog's toys (stuffed animals work best) into the pyramidal arrangement of bowling pins. You then roll a ball into the group, scattering the toys about and watching the dog try to figure out which to rescue first.

87. Water Taxi

Not every dog is a great swimmer, but that
doesn't mean they can't join in the fun.
Many dogs will stand or lay on an air mattress,
enjoying the pool without getting wet.
You may want to try getting your dog to walk
on the mattress while it's on solid ground
to get her used to the sensation.
So much better than being left poolside!

*NOTE: Of course, air mattresses and long nails don't mix! And please
don't let the dog near water without a lifeguard.*

88. Sockie Ball

Looking for something to do with all of
those socks that are mysteriously left without
their mates once going through the wash?
Roll them up and make a soft ball
to throw inside the house.

89. Courier Pigeon

Have a message to send to someone
in another room of the house?
Don't yell—attach a note to the dog
and send him on the errand: "Go find Daddy!"

90. Everybody Limbo!

Use a broom or mop handle as a limbo pole, and
limbo away! Be prepared for serious cheating.
Dogs will go under the handle stomach-down,
and when the going gets tough,
they usually give up and leap *over* the handle.

91. Hip-Hop

Hop up and down! One foot! Both feet!
Everyone!

92. Leap Frog

Here's a more elaborate variation on the simple hopping routine. Start in a squat or crouch, and spring upward in your best froggie impression. "Ribbits" are optional.

93. Chutes and Ladders

Some dogs will take advantage of the park's playground equipment and shimmy down the children's slide! Smaller dogs may prefer to ride on your lap. Whee!

94. Buried Treasure

Fill a large shallow box or old kiddie pool
with soil, and bury fun treats and toys
in the dirt. Natural diggers love to have
their own space to root around in.

95. Twist the Night Away

Dogs with short tails seem to be naturally adept at doing the Twist! Lacking a substantial tail, their whole rump wags and wiggles in an exaggerated expression.
Pop in a Chubby Checker album and twist away happily with your stub-tailed friend!

96. Patty-Cakes

When the dog is lying down, put one of your
hands on top of her paws. He will probably
pull it away and may put his paw on top
of your hand. Then you pull out your hand and
put it on top of his paw, and so on.

97. Hot Pursuit

Strap a stuffed animal on top of
a remote-controlled car, and let 'er rip!

NOTE: This is especially fun for racing or hunting breeds.

About the models:

 Ripley is a Samoyed of almost 15 years. She is a bundle of contradictions: loyal and flirty; graceful and clumsy; sweet and stubborn. She lives in New York City, and was named for the heroine of the *Alien* movies.

 Lucy is a Petit Basset Griffon Vendeen: a long, weird name for a long, weird dog! She was found as a stray in Brooklyn, New York, and astonishes her father with her empathy and love for everyone she meets.

 Benny is a 7-year-old Brittany spaniel living in New York City. He loves long walks in the park, where he searches for pigeons and squirrels.

 Cody is an 8-year-old Shepherd mix living in Virginia. He loves vanilla ice cream, snuggling, and barking at waves on the beach.

 Kato is a 9-year-old Boxer from Queens, New York. His favorite activities include sleeping on the couch and watching people pass outside the window.

 Sydney is a 7-year-old Australian cattle dog living in Brooklyn, New York. She loves herding pigeons, ducks, lazy dogs, and party guests. She collects shoes in her spare time.

Maxine is described by her mother as a "Jackahuahua": part Jack Russell and part Chihuahua. She is blessed with both beauty and brains, and is becoming the toast of the literary set; she has also appeared in a popular children's book.

 Atlas is an 8-year-old Beagle from New York. She loves napping under the covers, taking long walks, and snatching things off the street. She is skilled at catching ice cubes in her mouth.

 Blanca is a 3-year-old Yellow Lab. She lives in New York City, where her favorite pastime is shopping.

 Yonah is a Rottweiler from New York and New Jersey. A gentle giant, she has developed quite a fan base in her neighborhoods. She lives with her sister, Anya the cat; they take turns giving each other ear washes.

 Mya is a pug living on New York City's West Side, where she is the life of every party. Unlike other pugs' tongues, Mya's hangs straight out of her mouth and does not curl.

 Petrucchio is a 5-year-old spaniel who divides his time between New York City, Nantucket, and Palm Beach, Florida. He is an international traveler, who has had his likeness committed to Italian ceramic tiles. His favorite pastime is collecting biscuits from upscale boutiques and clothing stores.

 Trevi is 12 years old. He splits his time between New York City and Roxbury, Connecticut. He has attended the Jack Russell Nationals twice, and has won numerous racing ribbons. On weekends, he enjoys floating in the swimming pool and chasing wild turkeys.

 Audrey was born in November, 2002. She is an Italian greyhound from New York City, where she lives with one sibling: a parrot named Zelda. She smiles when there is a knock at the door, which generally means Chinese food (and shrimp dumplings).

 Grady is a 7-year-old Airedale. He follows the beat of his own drum and makes no apologies for being a "mama's boy."

 Chloë is a 2-year-old spaniel and the quintessential New York City girl. She insists on being acknowledged by anyone within reach.

 Biscuit is known for his fondness for beach balls, or any ball bigger than his head. A 3-year-old Pekingese, Biscuit lives in Brooklyn, New York.

Reese & Applejack are miniature poodles from New York City. Reese is the quiet, thoughtful brother. Applejack delights in noisily chasing squirrels and birds.

 Puppy is a 2-year-old Great Dane from New York. He has a jealous nature, and must be the center of attention at all times. He is very comfortable sitting in his mother's lap (ouch!), and is always free for a hug.

 Maisie is a yellow Lab–Chihuahua mix (don't ask!) from Brooklyn, New York. During the day, she naps and takes walks with her friend Sam; in the evening, she chews rawhide and snuggles.

 Henry is a 4-year-old French bulldog from New York, who has been dubbed "The Buddha of Greenwich Village." His needs are simple: his father, his soccer ball, and the sofa.

 Clyde is a Rhodesian Ridgeback. He helps run a clothing store, Spooly D's, in Greenwich Village, New York.

 Chloë is a 2-year-old beagle. She lives in New York City, where she loves to play with her stuffed ferret and be chased around the house. She is two years old.

Farnsworth (Farnie) is a 3 year old fox terrier living with his two human brothers, aged 5 and 7. His favorite activities include ball fetching, tug-of-war, and squirrel chasing.

 Mikey is a Brussels griffon. He is described as the sweetest, most gentle of souls. He even loves babies! He lovingly cares for his stuffed duck (which has seen better days) at his home in New York City.

 Misabella is a 4-year-old Maltese. An Aries, she keeps boyfriends in both New York and Florida. Misa is a registered Pet Partner and a devoted therapy dog.

 Lucy is a Rottweiler from New Jersey. When she isn't lounging in bed, she spends her days patrolling the windows for potentially dangerous passersby (the neighbors, stray cats, squirrels) and chasing her two feline housemates. Lucy, a Virgo, is currently single, but her best friend, a Bullmastiff named Moe, seems to be interested in more than just friendship.

 Rudi is a miniature pinscher from New York City. She watches the world go by from her perch on the couch.

Rocky is a 10-year-old boxer and pit bull mix from upstate New York. Quite the thief, he has been known to snatch everything from food to toilet paper. He also has a soft side: Rocky was the surrogate father to a litter of kittens.

 Teddy lives in New York City and is a shameless sock thief.

 Juandino (Dino) is a 12-year-old Pomeranian. He is an experienced traveler but makes his home in New York. His favorite foods include rice, chicken, and ice cream (not necessarily together).

 Mickey was rescued from the streets 2 years ago, and is now the honorary mayor of his neighborhood. He loves long walks and begging shamelessly for treats. He recently won the Kindest Face award at the Gramercy Park Dog Show in New York City.

 Jasper is a young Boykin spaniel from the Washington, D.C. area.

 Jake is a one-year-old Shiba Inu from New York. He is a daily fixture at his neighborhood dog park, where he loves playing with all dogs, large and small. On weekends, he hits the beach in New Jersey.

Lucy is Henry's bossy sister. She is a 3-year-old Boston terrier born in Florida but now living in New York City. She still loves to sunbathe.

 Lucy is a Chihuahua from New York. Always thinking ahead, Lucy likes to hide treats in her bed for later use. She loves belly rubs, long walks, and tackling the cats.

 Edie is a 4-year-old Welsh Pembroke corgi from New York City. Far swifter than her shape would imply, she is quite the speed demon. She loves herding people in group situations, and flirts shamelessly with men.

 Kane is a Chow/Labrador mix of 7 years. He lives in New York City, where he enjoys beachcombing and begging for steakhouse leftovers.

 Finbar is a 2-year-old golden retriever who, like many New Yorkers, prefers not to retrieve things but to have them delivered. He spends his weekends in a log cabin in the Catskills, where he is learning that chewing the walls is not appropriate behavior.

 Lucy is a Border collie mix from Larchmont, New York. She lives next to Ali and is his girlfriend.

JB is a 10-year-old bearded collie mix living in New York, where is completely and utterly devoted to his ball (which he cherishes above all else, even dinner).

Atticus is a 2-year-old pound puppy. He lives in New York City, where his mother is constantly chasing him out of the bathtub.

Neo is a 7-month-old Australian shepherd living in New York City. He spends most days accumulating admirers at his father's flower shop.

Ali is a boxer from Larchmont, New York, whose nickname is "The Gentleman."

Fuji is a young Pekingese and Shih Tzu cross from New York City. He carries his toys wherever he goes, and has a propensity for rolling over when other dogs come near.

Allegro is an 8-year-old Yorkie from New York. He has more personality than you think could fit into his five-pound body. An unapologetic couch potato, he loves to cuddle and sleep. He can often be found snoring, and even barking in his sleep.

Samantha is a Shih Tzu of a certain age—17 to be exact! Her hobbies include licking foreheads, sleeping, and her famous tissue trick. She was once winner of the Central Park Dog Show's Nicest Face award. She lives in New York.

 Lester is a 4-year-old Scottie born in Kansas, but raised in Philadelphia and Brooklyn. He enjoys chasing squirrels, biting toes, and licking carpets. Lester was named for a Buick dealership in New Jersey.

 Zevon is a 14-year-old wire terrier who loves diving into tree planters and snatching anything up from the sidewalk. He lives in New York City.

 Belle is a Sheltie from New York. She enjoys chasing rabbits in the country, while her sister Molly prefers rearranging the sock drawer.

 Carlito is an Italian greyhound and Chihuahua mix. A shelter dog with a sad and dubious past, he now lives in New York City where his monkey face never fails to illicit puzzled looks from passersby. The only thing he loves more than his pink "piggy" is his mother, whom he insists on protecting from roving bands of schoolchildren and the occasional nun.

Coco is an 11-year-old Lhasa Apso from New York. She is a proud fixture at her mother's pet boutique, Barkley, where she sits poised at the counter, happily greeting patrons.

 Geordie was born in Kansas City, Kansas in 1999. He now lives in New York City, where he refuses to be seen outdoors sporting anything less than a designer collar. He divides his time between the city and his country home, where he enjoys taking up all the bed space (quite a feat for a dog his size!).

 Parker (Teaulait's Parker Posey) is a 3-year-old vizsla from New York City. Always the life of the party, she loves to play with plastic soda bottles, and avoids the rain at all costs.

 Louis is a young chocolate Lab of just over one year, living in New York City. He loves to circulate between the pet shop, the park, the local firehouse, and the coffee shop.

Acknowledgments

This book would not exist without the inspiration of editor *par excellence*, Jennifer Griffin. Her dedication, persistence, patience, and belief in this project were inestimable.

Many thanks also to photographer Pat Doyle, Workman's Paul Gamarello, Leora Kahn, Cindy Schoen, Marta Jaremko, Katherine Adzima, Wayne Kirn, and Aaron Clendening, as well as all of the doggie models (and their people!). Their participation made this project not only possible, but happy and fun.

Special thanks to all of my dear friends at Blue Cross Pet Hospital and Lenox Hill Veterinarians.